6-15

Edith B. Siegrist
Vermillion Public Library
18 Church Street
Vermillion, SD 57069
(605) 677-7060

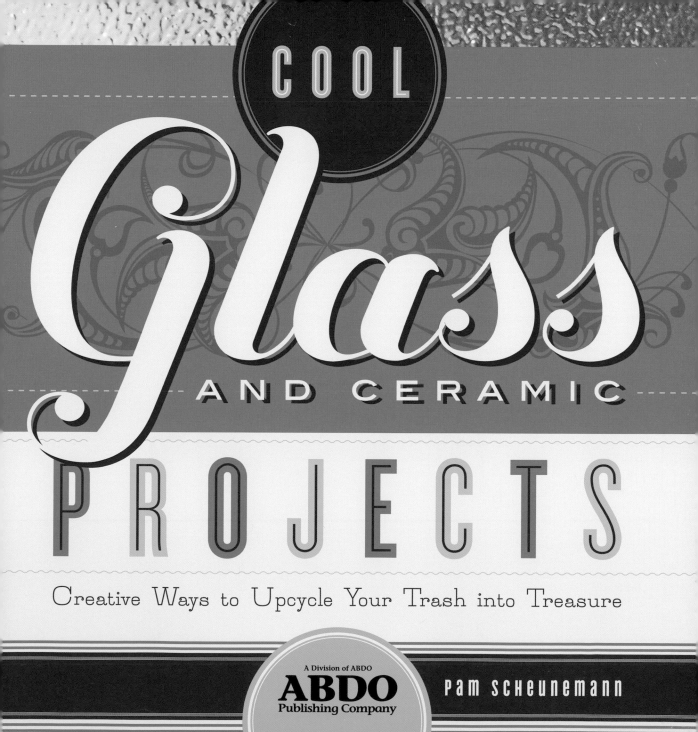

COOL

Glass

AND CERAMIC

PROJECTS

Creative Ways to Upcycle Your Trash into Treasure

A Division of ABDO
ABDO
Publishing Company

PAM SCHEUNEMANN

visit us at www.abdopublishing.com

Published by ABDO Publishing Company, a division of ABDO,
P.O. Box 398166, Minneapolis, Minnesota 55439. Copyright
© 2013 by Abdo Consulting Group, Inc. International
copyrights reserved in all countries. No part of this book may
be reproduced in any form without written permission from
the publisher. Checkerboard Library™ is a trademark and
logo of ABDO Publishing Company.

Printed in the United States of America, North Mankato,
Minnesota
062012
092012

 PRINTED ON RECYCLED PAPER

DESIGN AND PRODUCTION: ANDERS HANSON, MIGHTY MEDIA, INC.
SERIES EDITOR: LIZ SALZMANN
PHOTO CREDITS: SHUTTERSTOCK

The following manufacturers/names appearing in this
book are trademarks: Americana® Multi-Purpose™ Sealer,
Connoisseur Carnival, Creative Imaginations®, Glitter Glue™,
Goo Gone®, Krylon®, Mod Podge®, Painter's Mate Green®,
Rust-oleum®, Sharpie®, Singer®, Weldbond®

LIBRARY OF CONGRESS CATALOGING-IN-PUBLICATION DATA

Scheunemann, Pam, 1955-
  Cool glass and ceramic projects : creative ways to upcycle
your trash into treasure / Pam Scheunemann.
      p. cm. -- (Cool trash to treasure)
  Includes index.
  ISBN 978-1-61783-433-2
  1. Pottery craft--Juvenile literature. I. Title.
  TT921.S34 2013
  666'.3--dc23

                                          2011052199

TABLE of CONTENTS

TRASH TO *Treasure*

THE SKY'S THE LIMIT

The days of throwing everything in the trash are long over. Recycling has become a part of everyday life. To recycle means to use something again or to find a new use for it. By creating treasures out of trash, we are also *upcycling*. This is a term used to **describe** making useful items out of things that may have been thrown away.

Maybe you've been putting all your glass jars in the recycling bin. Why not take a fresh look at all those jars and give them new life? Glass jars are great for storing stuff. They are easily **available**. Everyone's got a few empty jars laying around. See what you can come up with. The sky's the limit.

Permission and Safety

- Always get **permission** before making any type of craft at home.

- Ask if you can use the tools and materials needed.

- Ask for help when you need it.

- Be careful when using knives, scissors, or other sharp objects.

- Be especially careful if you happen to break any glass.

Be Prepared

- Read the entire activity before you begin.

- Make sure you have everything you need to do the project.

- Keep your work area clean and organized.

- Follow the directions carefully.

- Clean up after you are finished for the day.

Some types of glass cannot be recycled. These include things such as dishes, vases and window glass. They contain materials that would spoil the recycling process. It is even more important to look for ways to upcycle these items.

In this book you'll find great ideas to upcycle different kinds of glass. Make them just like they appear here or use your own ideas. You can make them for yourself or as gifts for others. These projects use easy-to-find tools and materials.

GLASS

AND CERAMICS

Many everyday items are made of glass. Glass can be found all around us. It's in jars, bottles, plates, bowls, and more. Here are some ideas for reusing or upcycling glass and **ceramics**.

Glass Jars

Jars come in many sizes and colors. Here are some things they can be made into.

- VASES
- PIGGY BANKS OR CHANGE JARS
- STORAGE CONTAINERS
- CANDLE HOLDERS

Glassware and Ceramics

More than likely you have some unused glass items around your house. You can also go to **garage** sales and **thrift stores**. They often have a lot of glassware and **ceramics**. Some of it, such as vases, you may want to reuse as is. But you can also upcycle those pieces. There are some projects in this book that will show you how. Here are some things you can make.

- BIRD FEEDERS
- SERVING PLATES
- UNUSUAL PLANTERS

CLEANING THE GLASS

Glass jars often have labels that must be removed before you reuse them. Some labels come off easily and some take a bit more work. First wash the jar in hot, soapy water. Let it dry. If there is still glue on the jar, use Goo Gone to remove it. Sometimes it is hard to get off. Just have patience and keep at it. Wash the jar again in hot, soapy water.

TOOLS & MATERIALS

½-INCH (1 CM) COPPER CAP

½-INCH (1 CM) COPPER PIPE

ACRYLIC PAINT

ACRYLIC SEALER

ADHESIVE LETTERS

CARD STOCK

COASTER-SIZE TILES

COLORED CHALK

COLORED TISSUE PAPER

CONTACT PAPER

CORK

DECORATIVE GEMS

DECORATIVE HOLE PUNCH

DECORATIVE-EDGE SCISSORS

FOAM PAINTBRUSHES

FROSTED GLASS PAINT

GLASS JARS AND VASES

GLITTER GLUE

HOT GLUE GUN AND GLUE

LATEX CHALKBOARD PAINT

LED VOTIVE LIGHTS

MOD PODGE

PAINTBRUSH

PAINTER'S TAPE

PINS

RIBBON

SANDPAPER

STIR STICK

TEACUP AND SAUCER

TWO-PIECE CANNING JAR LID

VASES OR CANDLESTICK HOLDERS

WELDBOND

- **COLORED TISSUE PAPER**

- **DECORATIVE-EDGE SCISSORS**

- **STRAIGHT-SIDED GLASS VASE**

- **MOD PODGE**

- **FOAM PAINTBRUSH**

- **THICK PAPER**

- **DECORATIVE PAPER PUNCHES**

Save tissue paper from gifts you receive. You can reuse it in projects such as this one.

ALL WRAPPED UP

Makes a great candle holder or vase!

1. **Crumple** a piece of tissue paper. Then smooth it out. Fold it several times in the same direction. Use decorative-edge scissors to cut off the ends. Then cut along the folded edges.

2. Separate the strips of tissue paper. Cut the strips so that they fit around the vase. Make enough strips to cover the whole vase. Try using different colors.

3. Turn the vase upside down. Brush Mod Podge around the outside of the vase. Cover an area as wide as one of the tissue strips.

4. Wrap a strip around the vase over the Mod Podge. Smooth out any bubbles. It's okay if there are wrinkles. Spread more Mod Podge and add another strip below the first one. The strips should **overlap** a little bit. Repeat until the vase is covered with tissue paper. Let the Mod Podge dry.

5. Fold a piece of tissue paper into several layers. Put a piece of thick paper behind the tissue paper to keep it stiff. Use a decorative paper punch to make small shapes.

6. Glue the shapes onto the vase. Let the Mod Podge dry. Then cover the whole vase with another coat of Mod Podge. Let it dry.

STUFF YOU'LL NEED

- CARD STOCK
- MARKER
- SCISSORS
- CONTACT PAPER
- SMALL GLASS JAR
- ADHESIVE LETTERS OR STICKERS
- NEWSPAPER
- FROSTED GLASS PAINT
- VOTIVE LIGHT OR CANDLE

GLASS JAR LANTERN

Fabulous, frosty, flickering flames!

1. Draw a design on the card stock. It can be anything you like. Make sure it will fit on the jar. Cut out the design. You will use it as a pattern.

2. Lay the pattern on the back side of the contact paper. Trace around the pattern. Cut it out.

3. Peel the backing off the contact-paper design. Stick the design on the jar. Add adhesive letters or other stickers.

4. Spread newspaper out in an area with good **ventilation**. It's best to do this outside or in a **garage** if you can. Set the jar upside down on the newspaper. Spray the jar with frosted glass paint. Follow the directions on the spray can.

5. Let the paint dry completely. Remove the contact paper and stickers. If there is a little glue left, gently rub it with a wet paper **towel**. Be careful not to scratch the paint. Put a votive light in it and enjoy the glow!

Some stickers and contact paper are harder to remove than others. Test them on a different jar to make sure they will come off.

13

Crayons

Gems

Bea

14

REMARKABLE JAR

Change the label? No problem!

1. Use the painter's tape to make a border around the area you want to paint.

2. Spread newspaper over your work surface. Stir the paint. Paint the area inside the tape. Apply three coats. Let the paint dry between coats.

3. Let the last coat dry. Then carefully peel off the painter's tape.

4. Wait a few days to make sure the paint is completely dry. Then you can write on the painted area with chalk. Just erase the chalk when you need to change the label!

- **CANNING JAR WITH TWO-PIECE LID**
- **SCRAP OF FELT**
- **MARKER**
- **SCISSORS**
- **SCRAP OF FABRIC**
- **RULER**
- **COTTON BALLS**
- **GLUE**
- **PINS**

On Pins and Needles

Don't get stuck on this project!

1. The pieces of a canning jar lid are the flat lid and the band. Separate the lid and the band.

2. Place the lid on the felt. Trace around it with the marker. Cut out the felt circle.

3. Lay the fabric face down. Place the lid on the fabric. Trace around it with the marker.

4. Make several marks about 1 inch (3 cm) outside the circle. Draw a larger circle around the first circle by connecting the marks. Cut out the larger circle.

Continued on the next page

17

5 Lay the fabric circle face down. Put cotton balls on the fabric inside the smaller circle. Put the lid top down on top of the cotton balls.

6 Put the **stack** of the fabric, cotton balls, and lid in the band.

7 Press the lid into the band. The cotton balls and fabric will make a bump above the band. That's the pincushion! Pull the edges of the fabric to remove any wrinkles.

8. Make some small cuts in the edges of the fabric. Fold the edges over. Glue them to the back of the lid. Try to glue them as flat as possible.

9. Take the pincushion out of the band. Glue the felt circle to the back of the pincushion.

10. Put glue around the inside edge of the band. Put the pincushion back into the band. Press it firmly. Let the glue dry. Put the lid on the jar. Store supplies in the jar, and pins on top!

Try decorating your jar with stickers, buttons, or ribbons.

STUFF YOU'LL NEED

- **COASTER-SIZE TILE**

- **RULER**

- **DECORATIVE PAPER OR PHOTO**

- **SCISSORS**

- **MOD PODGE**

- **PAINTBRUSH**

- **ACRYLIC SEALER**

- **SHEET OF CORK**

- **HOT GLUE GUN AND GLUE**

TERRIFIC TILE COASTER

Set your drinks on terrific tiles!

1. Measure the tile. Cut the paper or photo 1/4 inch (.5 cm) smaller than the tile on each side.

2. Paint the top side of the tile with Mod Podge.

3. Put the paper or photo in the center of the tile. Smooth out any air bubbles.

4. Brush Mod Podge over the paper or photo and all the way to the edges of the tile. Let it dry. Cover the tile with another coat of Mod Podge. Let it dry.

5. Put a coat of acrylic sealer on the tile. Let it dry.

6. Cut a piece of **cork** the same size you cut the paper or photo. Have an adult help you use the hot glue gun. Glue the cork to the back of the tile.

21

- **GLASS JAR**
- **ACRYLIC PAINT**
- **RIBBON**
- **SCISSORS**
- **GLUE**
- **DECORATIVE GEMS**
- **GLITTER GLUE**

BOTTLE BLING

A creative container!

1. Pour acrylic paint into the jar. Gently **swirl** it around to cover the inside of the jar. Add more paint if necessary. When the entire inside of the jar is coated, pour out the extra paint. Let it dry.

2. Cut a piece of ribbon to fit around the jar. Glue the ribbon around the jar.

3. Lay the jar on its side. Put a dab of glitter glue on the jar. Press a gem into the glue. Add more gems to the side of the jar facing up. Let the glue dry. Then turn the jar to add gems to another side.

> Glitter glue takes a long time to dry. It can run if the jar is not lying flat.

23

STUFF YOU'LL NEED

- TEACUP AND SAUCER
- SANDPAPER
- WELDBOND
- HEAVY BOOK
- METAL SPOON
- ½-INCH COPPER PIPE CAP
- ½-INCH COPPER PIPE, 4 FEET (1.2 M) LONG
- BIRDSEED

Tea Time for Birds

Invite some birds to a tea party!

1   Wash and dry the teacup and saucer.

2   Lightly sand the bottom of the teacup.
    Then sand the top of the saucer. Only
    sand the middle, where the teacup sits.
    Sanding helps the glue hold better.

3   Turn the teacup upside down. Apply
    Weldbond to the part that touches the
    saucer.

4   Press the teacup firmly onto the saucer.
    Put a book on top of the cup. This will
    keep the teacup in place while the
    Weldbond is drying.

Continued on the next page

5. Sand the underside of the spoon. Sand the saucer where you want the spoon to sit.

6. Put some Weldbond on the underside of the spoon. Press the spoon firmly in place. Keep pressing for a minute or two. It is very important for the Weldbond to dry completely. Check the label and wait as long as it says to.

7. When the glue is completely dry, turn the teacup upside down. Sand a 1/2-inch (1 cm) circle in the middle.

8   Sand the top of the copper pipe cap. Put glue on the top of the cap.

9   Press the cap to the bottom of the saucer. Wait for the Weldbond to completely dry. Don't do the next step before it is dry.

10 Stick one end of the copper pipe in the ground. Make sure it won't tip easily. Put the teacup and saucer on top of the pipe using the copper pipe cap. Fill the teacup with birdseed and let the birds enjoy!

- CERAMIC BOWL

- 2 CERAMIC PLATES, DIFFERENT SIZES

- CERAMIC CANDLE HOLDER OR VASE

- WELDBOND

- HEAVY BOOK

cute cupcake tiers

Give old dishes new life!

1. Wash and dry the bowl, plates, and candle holder.

2. Turn the bowl upside down. Put Weldbond on the bottom of the bowl.

3. Put the larger plate on the upside-down bowl. The plate should be right-side up. Be sure it is centered on the bowl.

4. Hold it in place for a minute. Put a heavy book on top to hold it down. Let the Weldbond dry completely. Follow the instructions on the label.

5. Put Weldbond on the bottom of the candle holder. Place it in the center of the plate. Repeat step 4.

6. Put Weldbond on the top of the candle holder. Put the smaller plate on it. Make sure it is centered. Repeat step 4.

7. Use your cupcake **tiers** to serve cupcakes or other treats!

CONCLUSION

Now you know what upcycling is all about. What hidden gems do you have around your house? Do you have relatives who need their **attic** cleaned? What about **garage** and yard sales? Are there **thrift stores** and reuse centers near you? These are all great sources for materials that you can upcycle!

There are many benefits to upcycling. You can make some really great stuff for yourself or gifts for your family and friends. You can save useful things from going into the trash. And the best part is, you don't have to spend a lot of money doing it!

So keep your eyes and ears open for new ideas. There are many Web sites that are all about recycling and upcycling. You might find ideas on TV or in magazines. There are endless ways that you can make something beautiful and useful from **discarded** materials. Remember, the sky's the limit!

GLOSSARY

ATTIC – a room right under the roof of a building.

AVAILABLE – able to be had or used.

CERAMIC – something made out of clay that is baked at high temperatures to become very hard.

CORK – a material made out of tree bark.

CRUMPLE – to crush or bend something out of shape.

DESCRIBE – to tell about something with words or pictures.

DISCARD – to throw away.

GARAGE – a room or building that cars are kept in. A *garage sale* is a sale that takes place in a garage.

OVERLAP – to lie partly on top of something.

PERMISSION – when a person in charge says it's okay to do something.

STACK – a pile of things placed one on top of the other.

SWIRL – to whirl or to move smoothly in circles.

TIER – one of two or more rows, layers, or levels.

THRIFT STORE – a store that sells used items, especially one that is run by a charity.

TOWEL – a cloth or paper used for cleaning or drying.

VENTILATION – the movement of air through a room or other space.

Web sites

To learn more about cool craft projects, visit ABDO Publishing Company on the World Wide Web at www.abdopublishing.com. Web sites about creative ways for upcycling trash are featured on our Book Links page. These links are routinely monitored and updated to provide the most current information available.

INDEX